SMARTS!
Everybody's Got Them

Thomas Armstrong, Ph.D.

Illustrated by Tim Palin

free spirit
PUBLISHING®

Library of Congress Cataloging-in-Publication Data
Names: Armstrong, Thomas, author. | Palin, Tim, illustrator.
Title: Smarts! : everybody's got them / Thomas Armstrong ; illustrated by Tim Palin.
Description: Minneapolis : Free Spirit Publishing, [2019] | Audience: Age: 5–9.
Identifiers: LCCN 2018059004| ISBN 9781631983665 (hard cover 13) | ISBN 1631983660 (hard cover 10) | ISBN 9781631983672 (Web PDF) |
    ISBN 9781631983689 (ePub)
Subjects: LCSH: Creative ability—Juvenile literature. | Knowledge—Juvenile literature.
Classification: LCC BF408 .A65 2019 | DDC 153.3/5—dc23 LC record available at https://lccn.loc.gov/2018059004

Free Spirit Publishing does not have control over or assume responsibility for author or third-party websites and their content.

Reading Level Grade 2; Interest Level Ages 5–9;
Fountas & Pinnell Guided Reading Level M

Edited by Brian Farrey-Latz
Cover and interior design by Emily Dyer

10 9 8 7 6 5 4 3 2 1
Printed in China
R18860819

Free Spirit Publishing Inc.
6325 Sandburg Road, Suite 100
Minneapolis, MN 55427-3674
(612) 338-2068
help4kids@freespirit.com
freespirit.com

Free Spirit offers competitive pricing.
Contact edsales@freespirit.com for pricing information on multiple quantity purchases.

For Maddie and Ollie

Everyone is smart in lots of ways.

Or if people
make fun of you.

But the truth is, your brain is full of lots of **different kinds** of smarts!

Here are ways that everyone is smart—**including you.**

learn a craft
like woodworking
or knitting

play sports

make things
with clay

. . . you exercise your BODY SMARTS.

go camping

watch birds

recycle trash

. . . you use your **NATURE SMARTS.**

You can do lots of things to get smarter in each of these different ways.

WORD

MUSIC

NUMBER

PICTURE

BODY

PEOPLE

SELF

NATURE

But smarts don't just fall from the sky.

Smarts need you to help them along.

Smarts are like our bodies.

They can **grow stronger** the more they're used.

And they can **grow weaker** the less we use them.

Some smarts **grow** **faster** than others.

Maybe you like using words more than you like doing math.

But you can be smart in **BOTH** ways if you work at it!

The more you draw images, the more your **picture smarts** can grow.

NATURE SMARTS

The more you study different kinds of plants, the more your **nature smarts** can grow.

This is true for every kind of smarts you have. And **you have them all!**

Making mistakes is another way to get smarter.

That's right! Even when you sing a wrong note
or miss catching a fly ball, you can learn from it.

When you do, you're getting smarter, so you'll do better next time.

You can be as smart as you want in lots of different ways!
The more you like something and the more you work at it, the smarter you can get.

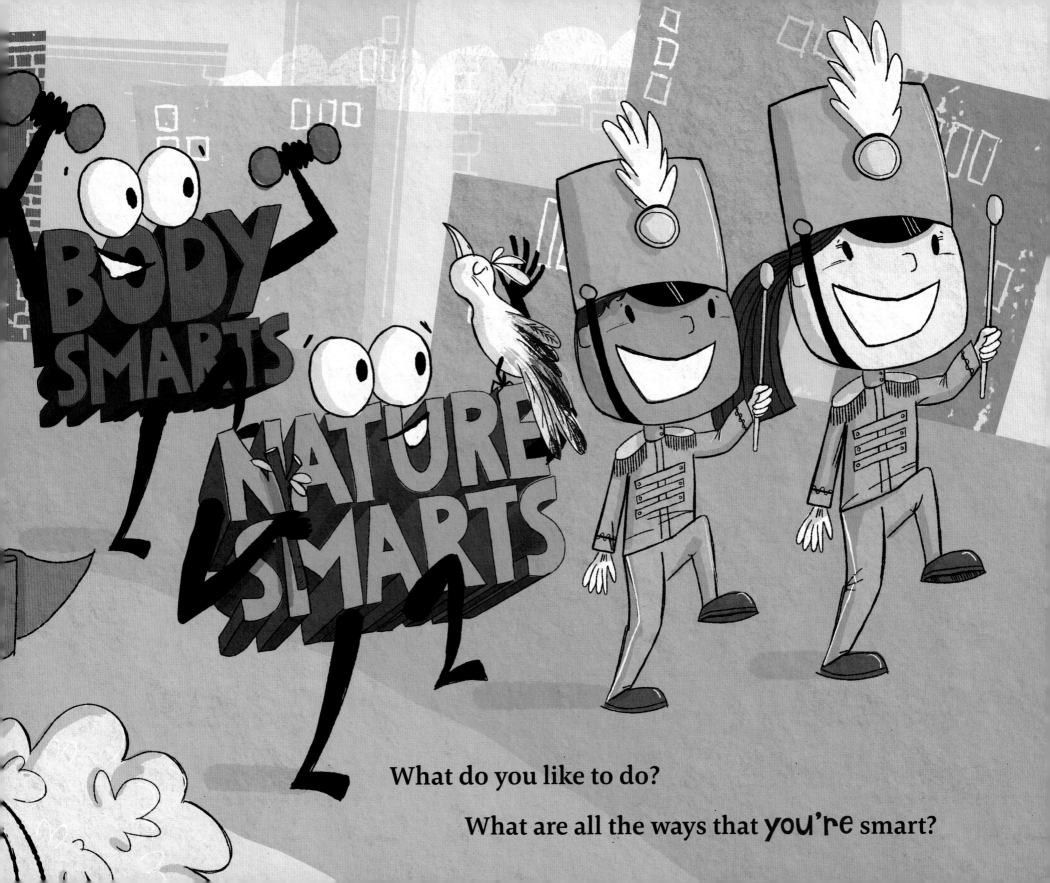

What do you like to do?

What are all the ways that YOU'RE smart?

The ideas in this book are based on the theory of multiple intelligences, first presented in 1983 by Howard Gardner, a professor of education at Harvard University. Gardner identified eight separate intelligences that everyone has: word smarts, music smarts, number smarts, picture smarts, body smarts, people smarts, self smarts, and nature smarts. This theory not only helps explain a wide range of ways in which children learn but also suggests practical methods for developing learning tools to help them succeed.

All children are unique in the way the eight intelligences function in their brains. Most kids are highly developed in one or two intelligences, moderately developed in two or three others, and relatively little developed in one or two more. It's most effective to identify a child's most highly developed intelligences first, build confidence in those areas, and then use these intelligences to help strengthen less developed areas.

For example, to help a student who shows drawing abilities (a picture smarts skill) but has difficulty with reading (a word smarts skill), you could provide highly illustrated books such as graphic novels or picture books. Another powerful strategy is to build vocabulary by associating unfamiliar or challenging words with images. Similarly, you might try developing reading comprehension by taking photos of objects or scenes that help illustrate some of the main ideas of a text and showing these to students as they read. A student who is adept at physical activities (a body smarts skill) but has difficulty with adding and subtracting (number smarts skills) might walk along a number line taped to the floor, moving forward to add numbers and backward to subtract numbers. Or a child who has difficulty with learning new vocabulary words but loves to draw might illustrate the meaning of each new word with a vivid picture.

It's crucial that all kinds of smarts are developed *for their own sake*, not only to strengthen weaker areas. As often as possible, provide resources that allow kids to engage in activities spanning all eight intelligences. Many curricula offer natural tie-ins to certain smarts, such as English language arts to word smarts, math to number smarts, and physical education to body smarts. It may be necessary, though, to be creative when there are no clear connections between an intelligence and the curriculum, or if the curriculum is in some way lacking. For instance, if your school doesn't have a music program, you could play soft music during reading or quiet working times so kids can listen and analyze. If your school doesn't have an arts program, incorporate visual learning into everyday curricula by allowing students to draw pictures that demonstrate their comprehension of concepts being taught.

In other areas of the curriculum, you can brainstorm ways to expand instruction beyond fundamental skills and ideas. Math instruction can include rich real-world examples, including architecture, statistics in the news, and the mathematics of living forms (such as the dimensions of the chambered nautilus shell, which follow a numerical pattern called the Fibonacci sequence). Physical education activities can go beyond jumping jacks and dodgeball to include activities such as weight training, yoga, and rock climbing. The possibilities are vast!

Outside of school, parents and guardians can engage the whole family in activities that develop the intelligences by visiting places where the smarts are emphasized, such as:

> libraries (word smarts)

> indoor and outdoor musical concerts (music smarts)

> science museums, shopping centers, or grocery stores (number smarts)

> sculpture gardens, outdoor murals, or art museums (picture smarts)

> playgrounds, basketball courts, swimming pools, bowling alleys, or miniature golf courses (body smarts)

> community centers or neighborhood activities (people smarts)

> meditation groups or places of worship or spirituality (self smarts)

> parks, trails, urban gardens, zoos, or aquariums (nature smarts)

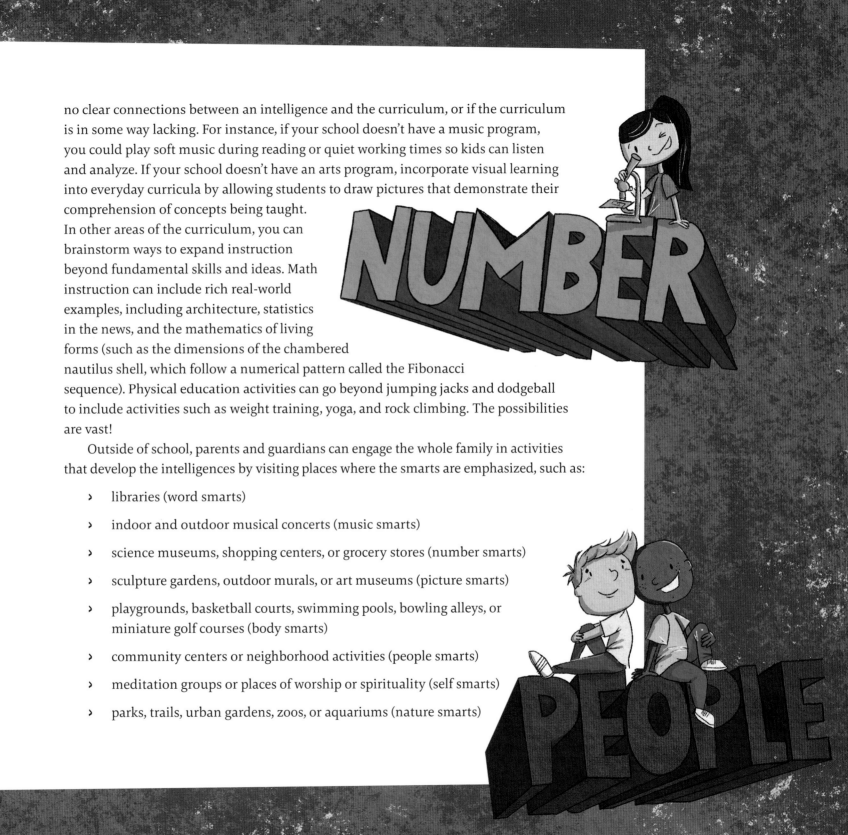

Families can also create activities at home to develop the intelligences, including:

> › a storytelling night (word smarts)

> › a sing-along night (music smarts)

> › a family math night where family members solve brainteasers from the newspaper or do math activities from a book such as *Family Math* by Jean Kerr Stenmark, Virginia Thompson, and Ruth Cossey (number smarts)

> › an art get-together where all the members of the family draw, paint, sculpt, or create some other kind of visual art (picture smarts)

> › a sports weekend (body smarts)

> › a family meeting or family council where issues affecting the family (such as a conflict, a future activity, or household chores) are discussed and resolved (people smarts)

> › group journaling (self smarts)

> › a walk together outdoors observing wildlife or plant life (nature smarts)

In addition, families can play games and work on puzzles together that develop various kinds of smarts, including:

> › anagrams, acrostics, or crossword puzzles (word smarts)

> › Name That Tune, in which someone sings, whistles, or hums three or four notes of a song and the group guesses what it is (music smarts)

> › games involving play money or other financial concepts, or puzzles such as sudoku (number smarts)

> › picture puzzles or picture-drawing group games (picture smarts)

> › hopscotch or four square, or small three-dimensional puzzles (body smarts)

> › conversation-based noncompetitive games such as Animal, Vegetable, Mineral or 20 Questions (people smarts)

> › games such as Would You Rather? that encourage reflection (self smarts)

> › a nature scavenger hunt where family members look for as many different plants, insects, or animals in their neighborhood as they can (nature smarts)

Apps and other technology can also be useful tools that provide opportunities for families and classrooms to build and expand all types of smarts. Some of these include:

> › speech-to-text apps that allow users to write stories, poems, essays, and reports by speaking (word smarts)

> › tools that allow kids to compose music electronically and explore harmonies, musical structure, and more (music smarts)

> › logic puzzle and brainteaser apps that require analytical thinking and problem-solving (number smarts)

> › drawing, painting, and photography apps that exercise artistic capabilities (picture smarts)

> › interactive, motion-sensing video games such as simulated table tennis, archery, or basketball that help develop physical skills (body smarts)

> › online communication including email, or file-sharing or collaborative platforms that can be used to start projects with other kids (people smarts)

> › simulation or role-play apps where players create personalities or avatars (self smarts)

> › ecological or environmental awareness apps or nature learning apps (nature smarts)

For students who have special needs (such as autism spectrum disorders, ADHD, or dyslexia), the exploration of multiple intelligences provides a wonderful way to focus on learners' individual and unique strengths. Kids diagnosed with autism spectrum disorders often display remarkable number smarts, for instance, while those identified as having dyslexia may show highly developed abilities in the area of three-dimensional picture smarts. Students diagnosed with ADHD may show body smarts or picture smarts capabilities, and so on. Identifying these qualities in all students can be an important part of helping them think about what they want to do, be, and achieve, including in their eventual careers—in part because the people who are happiest as adults often hold jobs where their responsibilities match their most developed (or most loved) intelligences. For this and many other reasons, it's essential for caring adults to provide a broad range of activities that will make it possible for all learners to thrive in each of the intelligences. Giving each child exposure to all the intelligences can help them realize their full potential and grow and develop into confident, healthy, and happy adults.

About the Author and Illustrator

Thomas Armstrong, Ph.D., is an award-winning author and speaker with forty years of teaching experience and 1.4 million copies of his books in print (translated into twenty-eight different languages). He has authored nineteen books, including *Multiple Intelligences in the Classroom* and *You're Smarter Than You Think: A Kid's Guide to Multiple Intelligences*; written numerous articles for *Parenting, Ladies' Home Journal, Family Circle,* and other periodicals; and appeared on several national and international television and radio programs, from NBC's *Today* show to the BBC. You can find Thomas's website at institute4learning.com. He lives in the Twin Cities in Minnesota.

Tim Palin has worked as a promotional art director for *ELLEgirl* magazine and senior designer for Disney Editions/Disney Press. He currently designs and produces books for children's publishers including Cantata Learning, Scholastic Books, and Blue Apple Books, and also illustrates books for children and tweens. Tim lives in Shirley, Massachusetts.

Other Great Books from Free Spirit

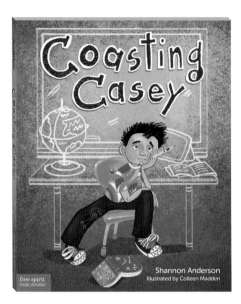

Coasting Casey
A Tale of Busting Boredom in School
by Shannon Anderson, illustrated by Colleen Madden
For ages 5–9. 48 pp.; PB and HC; color illust.; 8" x 10".

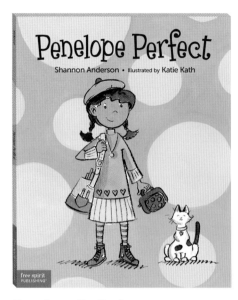

Penelope Perfect
A Tale of Perfectionism Gone Wild
by Shannon Anderson, illustrated by Katie Kath
For ages 5–9. 48 pp.; PB and HC; color illust.; 8" x 10".

I'm Happy-Sad Today
Making Sense of Mixed-Together Feelings
by Lory Britain, Ph.D., illustrated by Matthew Rivera
For ages 3–8. 40 pp.; HC; color illust.; 11¼" x 9¼".

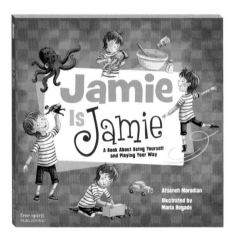

Jamie Is Jamie
A Book About Being Yourself and Playing Your Way
by Afsaneh Moradian, illustrated by Maria Bogade
For ages 4–8. 32 pp.; HC; color illust.; 8" x 8".

I Can Learn Social Skills
Poems About Getting Along, Being a Good Friend, and Growing Up
by Benjamin Farrey-Latz
For ages 5–9. 64 pp.; PB; color illust. & photos; 8" x 8".